KW-093-256

A TRAVELLER
FROM
STRATFORD

and other Poems

Also by Peter Leyland:
The Naked Mountain, William Heinemann (1951)

Poetry Library

113974

Li**t**e**r**a**t**u**r**e

THE POETRY LIBRARY

Literature Office, Royal Festival Hall,
South Bank Centre, London SE1 8XX

Telephone 071 921-0943

Open 7 days a week 11am - 8pm

Books may be renewed by telephone

Date due back

1 5 DEC 2001

A TRAVELLER FROM STRATFORD

and other Poems

Peter Leyland

POETRY LIBRARY
SOUTH BANK CENTRE
ROYAL FESTIVAL HALL
LONDON
SE1 8XX

BG

The Book Guild Ltd.
Sussex, England

This book is sold subject to the condition that it shall not, by way
of trade or otherwise, be lent, re-sold, hired out, photocopied or
held in any retrieval system, or otherwise circulated without the
publisher's prior consent in any form of binding or cover other than
that in which this is published and without a similar condition
including this condition being imposed on the subsequent purchaser.

15|5|95

The Book Guild Limited
25/26 High Street
Lewes, Sussex

First published 1991
© Peter Leyland 1991

Set in Bembo
Typeset by Hawks Phototypesetters Limited
Copthorne, West Sussex

Made and printed in Great Britain
by Antony Rowe Limited
Chippenham, Wiltshire

British Library Cataloguing in Publication Data
Leyland, Peter
    A Traveller from Stratford and other poems.
    I. Title
821.914
ISBN 0 86332 546 7

For
Apple
and
Celia

Acknowledgements

Some of the poems in this volume have been previously published in *The Naked Mountain* (William Heinemann 1951), *The Spectator* and *Time and Tide*.

Contents

from
THE
NAKED
MOUNTAIN

Tavistock Publications

THE WOOD

In woods in June I stand disconsolate,
While like a man who sees beneath smooth flesh
The skeleton's crudities, my thoughts explore
Earth's framework and that new-found world unseen
Which is the basis of the world we know.
But whose mind's eye can see, or pencil draw,
That dim fantastic subterranean world
Of symbols and of abstract formulæ,
Remote, impalpable, which lies within
That girl's soft cheek, the petals of this rose?
Then from that world infinitesimal,
From proton and electron, turn my thoughts
To sun and moon and the broad skies of night,
Seeking to trace that structure universal,
That scheme of which the fugitive galaxies
Are particles; but once again I find
A world impervious to imagination
In which terrestrial time and stellar space,
Summed in one vast and complex curvature,
Lose their identity, a world expressed
In cosmical equations, not in words.
   Entranced by sunbeams on the burnished leaves,
I turn back to the bright familiar wood,
Seeing the verdant earth, as the king saw
That torchlit hall through which the swallow flew—
As a brief interval of light and life
Dividing two intolerable worlds
Which man can never picture, never love.

THE POETRY LIBRARY

NIGHT OFF
NEWFOUNDLAND

Motionless all the night in fogbound seas
Where the wave swirling laps on floe and berg,
The ship lies to, until black sea and sky
From double gloom of mist and moonless midnight
Change with the dawn to frigid grey. Afar
Europe awaits us; but to-night my thoughts
Relinquish those rich landscapes, harmonies
Of primitive beauty and of agelong labour,
That soil where Nature seems no alien power
Indifferent or inimical to man.
On new immensities my memory dwells:
Again, in the clear daybreak of the north,
The violet mountains, rounded into domes,
Rise from the brown surge of the estuary
Whose farther bank the smooth horizon hides;
And in my thought I traverse prairie and desert,
Regions immense, void of sublimity,
Where, like a proud and newly conquered nation
Playing the host to foreign bayonets,
Nature submits, compelled by fire and steel
To render hospitality to man.
There fades the mind's inveterate dream, the haunting
Sense of an unseen power beneficient
To creatures she has made: for Nature seems
Motiveless in an unfamiliar vastness,
And that indwelling spirit of love and wisdom
Divined among the fells and tarns, in dale
And copse, or worshipped on Italian shores,
Eludes us in the illimitable expanse
Of forest, lake and prairie without end,
Lost in that continental spaciousness.

Yet for those lands wide and impersonal
Gladly would I exchange this fog, this gloom,
Cold seas interminable from Pole to Pole,
The slanting deck slippery with drizzling rain,
And the icy breeze that blows from the tall bergs
Drifting unseen around us. On this deck
Man feels no friendship, but hostility,
A cold immense malevolence, distilled
From all the works of Nature. What smooth mere
Luminous in twilight, what pine-stems red at sunset,
What olives poised above anemones,
May lure once more to confident trust in Nature
One who has known the ocean and the fog,
The loveless wilderness of the earth?

RECOLLECTIONS
AT DAWN

Around me on this hill
Trees don their greenery
And gorse its pallor of gold;
And I reflect how once
The leaves, the dew, the sky,
Would have entranced my mind
And would have left no sense unsatisfied.
No further joy I craved
Than to observe the long
Curve of a cherry-branch
Encrusted with white blossom; to admire
The last pine of the moor
In which the mountain gusts
Made solitary music; or to stand
On a darkening ridge of downs
Where sparse the beeches grew
Beyond whose stems the sun
Set, while the moon rose large from misty plains.

But now no rising moon,
Doubling the mysteries
Of dusk, no light of dawn,
Can satisfy a mind
Long sterile, which has grown
Conscious at last of its sterility.
No more content to enjoy
The tangible earth, it craves
A different world created by itself:—
Blossoming trees that flower
Rooted in lyrical thought;
Sequestered hills, devised
In the artist's ecstasy;
Moonrise on subtle twilights of the mind;
Grey peaks at dawn which owe
Neither to ice nor sun
Their wild diversity of dome and spire.

LONDON IN WARTIME

Between the broken roof-tree and the rafter
Jutting abruptly, helplessly, aloft,
That gold unreasonable serenity,
Bright in the ruins, must be Jupiter;
The sharp V of the mounting Hyades,
Red-tipped, points outward from the roof; and higher
That is no searchlight-pool, but hazed and blurred
The Pleiades; below, a jagged beam
Slants dark across Orion; and still lower
The random curve of the sagging masonry,
Fixed in its instantaneous cataract,
Concave and black, cradles the blue of Sirius.
And is this peace, the darkness of this ruin,
This lattice-work of stars, revisited
Between the bombs and the bombs? Nearer to peace
Than that long night when round us glared the fires,
Ourselves immune, till the shrill screech and roar
When all was flying glass and settling dust.
Then the relief, the sharp exhilaration,
Momentary, before the search that found
Wrecked corridors, a building torn and splintered,
And that one pitiful pool of blood which lay
Dark in the torchlight; roofless furnaces,
Glaring aloft their message of a hit,
While one by one we raked them; and above,
The skies that peered at us, noisy with engines,
Garish from searchlights; changing pools of light,
And the loose puffs of silver smoke that drifted
Slowly from star to star; and still, the stars,
Alone detached, alone immovable,
Partakers of man's ancient peace—how else
Then could we think of them? And in my head
Fancies of peace—leaves, hills, and isles—until
Old lines re-wrote themselves to an old tune:—

And we shall have some bombs there, for bombs come
dropping slow,
Dropping through the veils of evening to where the
siren sings;
The third floor's all a glimmer, the fourth a purple glow,
And the night-sky full of the bombers' wings.

And now this ruin, waiting for the sirens
Strangely delayed to-night: but afterwards,
Beyond this year, and next, shall we not see
These works of man, which man's work has destroyed,
Rebuilt? Where old Corinthian pillars towered,
New walls rise smoothly?—since man's nature is
Sometimes to ruin, always to create.
And what of those invulnerable stars,
So speciously secure—yet on this night,
While still the siren does not sound, while thought
Has leisure, how deny to their infection
A sad and puzzled, half-incredulous pity?
To-night, in star and planet, I perceive,
Beyond the wrecked roof and the shivered walls,
The emblems of a more profound decay,
Contingent on no human act, which works
Inherent in the atoms, and pervades
The constellations with a slow corruption;
And as I trace in thought that cosmic scheme,
Disintegrating, flawed from the foundation,
I see the intricate symmetry undone
And all that bright celestial architecture
Crumbling unalterably into ruin,
Dismantled, star by star, atom by atom,
Until the irreparable universe
Dissolves, to leave an orbless void of Space
And the idle flow of unregarded Time.

KEW GARDENS

Single, from the serried wood withdrawn,
Spring by the lake the deciduous cypresses,
Where the trees that make gloomier the swamps of Florida
   Throw their shadowy spires upon the lawn.

Silver through the brown oaks, birches gleam,
Not stunted as those that in twilit immensity
Look out on the cold and the slime of Siberia,
   Far from path and underwood and stream.

Sand and rock and prickly pear create,
Housed under glass, this desert innocuous
Where none die of thirst, and no boulder of Mexico
   Rattles with the warning heard too late.

Watch, and let your eyes delight, but know
This is not Earth, this peace and this harmony,
More than is Shakespeare revealed in anthologies
   Winnowed till his thoughts no longer show,

Purged of all life's agony and fear,
The lust and the hatred that mutter in Caliban,
Desdemona betrayed, Macbeth turned murderer,
   And the horror of the world of Lear.

IN THE GORGE
OF THE NIAGARA

Risen in the snowfields and highlands of the Arctic,
  Gathered from the prairie where the slow streams creep,
Smoothly from the great lakes flooding toward the ocean,
Out of misty Erie, far-sundering the forests,
  Foamless the waters of Niagara sweep.

Spreading through lagoons soft-brimming with the sunset,
  Curved bays mirroring the planets and the pines,
Circling the islands in a hundred mazy channels,
Flows the Niagara, like any other river,
  Till toward the gorge the river-shelf inclines.

Fiercer and narrower, cloudy-white with flung spray,
  Surf-lines breaking in their loose cascades of snow,
Downward through the rapids where the rock-bed steepens,
Closing on the sheer cliff, the river in its thundering
  Pours to the tumult of the cataract below.

Deep plunge the waters, and deep below the surface
  Journeying unseen the mighty current flows,
Twisting as the gorge twists, and rises in its onrush
Surging at the cliff-foot where the whole flood whitens,
  Pent in the chasm where the precipices close.

Blindly through the narrows, dense and straight and heavy,
    Drives the gathered weight of the waters of the west,
Vaulted to mid-stream with the fury of their onset,
Crowned with the foam of the everlasting breaker
    Heaving to the starlight a white tumultuous crest.

So may an artist, prodigal of labour, .
    Seeking to express all that senses may perceive,
Turn to one channel every current of his genius,
Patiently renouncing all that lures him to failure,
    Careless of success that another could achieve,

Holding to the one thing loved with power and passion,
    Searching for that form which none but he can find,
Till from all that loveliness he turned from creating,
Born in his fumbling, disillusion and frustration,
    Breaks a desperate grandeur, undesired and blind.

CECILY

Now is my long love over, and now fails
That passionate synthesis which she alone
Upon this world's diversity imposes;
Now must all things I hear and touch and see
Resume identity,
Denuded of all beauty save their own;
The moonlit downs, when June's long twilight closes,
Throb with no music but the nightingale's,
And once again the rose-tree bears but roses.

★　★　★

ST ANTONY
IN THE DESERT

Stars that through the Egyptian nights
   Orb by coloured orb succeed,
Lure the abstract mind to heights
   Where terrestrial dreams recede.

Whilst the restless sand is blown,
   Black each rib of rock remains,
Rigid as the changeless bone
   Under man's tumultuous veins.

Stars and rock presage the peace
   Promised long, and yet unknown,
When the mutinous flesh will cease
   Conflict with the mind and bone.

THE DREAM
OF GUINEVERE

This is the dream which came to me last night,
  Lancelot: I dreamt I cried in fear to you,
"How can we hope through love to find delight?
  When all our love is sin, what can we do?"

You said: "We can but sin, and then but die,
  And then there is but hell, for you and me—
That matchless place where both of us shall lie,
  Enchanted hell, where you and I will be.

God cannot touch this love of ours, which still
  Far in mid hell will ring us round with bliss.
Damned into rapture by His blundering will,
  How we shall mock His madness in a kiss!"

But in my dream God listened to your word,
  And sent down Uriel to chastise our sin:
'Go, slay them both; let all hell's fires be stirred
  To flare up round her as you fling her in.

His sin is worse than hers. Bodily pain
  Would but remit the anguish he must bear.
Build a fair mansion; there let him remain,
  Unscathed, in heaven, the heaven she shall not share.

Prepare his place for him; but give him not
  The power to make one piteous memory fade,
Till he shall pray those eyes may be forgot
  Which deep in heaven a haunted hell have made.

Her recompense of fire let him know well;
  She may take comfort, knowing him in heaven;
But bear him word that evermore in hell
  She burns beyond all hope of being forgiven.

Such is his punishment: so he shall stay
  In heaven, although he crave for hell and her;
In heaven, alone; in heaven, but far away,
  Throughout eternity, from Guinevere."

ON THE ATHENIAN FESTIVAL
OF DIONYSUS

When asphodel flushed the grey Acropolis,
In barbarous woodlands and by Scythian tents
Began the rituals of the fertile earth,
And Athens kept her spring-tide festival.
Far were Prometheus' scorn, Electra's grief,
Far from those primal rites where all began:
Winter interred with savage chants and blood,
Obscene and monstrous imagery of spring.

So may the mind, with its indigenous throng
Of racial memories—instincts unreclaimed—
Abhorred desires lying too deep to purge—
Transform some lust primeval and grotesque,
Till it shall yield, on canvas or in verse,
The Athenian beauty of an ordered art.

FIRST LOVE

Today has that girl's face
Recalled forgotten years
When new-born love bewildered all my mind;
But now that earliest love
Remote and alien seems,
Faded too far for thought to recollect:
Elusive as a scent
Enjoyed once, long ago,
Which leaves in the foiled mind
A sense of pleasure lost
Which even in memory cannot be restored.

★ ★ ★

IN EARLY SPRING

Now the remembered lark-notes from the blue
    Fall, and in woods familiar colours peep,
While, lest the spring should offer nothing new,
    The scents revive which memory could not keep.

ON THE MURDER OF MANDEL

JULY, 1944

Not only for the faith which others shared
That France could never die;
Nor for the courage that declined escape,
Choosing the fortress with its cell, and life
Contingent on the firmness of Pétain,
The honour of Laval;
Not only for the wit amid disaster,
The mockery that spared
No Frenchmen, only France;
The hope that did not doubt the Norman beaches,
The tricolour fluttering free,
And over German dead the Marseillaise:
Not only for these things
Men will recall his name,
But for this moment which his murderers choose:
As though, in the Eastern garden by the grave
Where of the Twelve not one had faith to wait,
Confident through the days and nights of death
Some lonely watcher had remained, to perish
As the earth shakes, and the stone rolls away,
The guard dispersing throw their weapons down,
And by that open tomb
The angel of the resurrection stands.

THE NAKED MOUNTAIN

Nanga Parbat ("Naked Mountain")—26,650 feet

Sharp on the skyline curves the distant ridge
Where on the crest the labouring Indians paused,
Wondering no more what drew the climbers higher,
As the last vapour-belt dissolved, and showed,
Too sheer for drift of snow or river of ice,
The mightiest mountain-wall from Pole to Pole
Plunging through mile on mile of vertical altitude
Down to the coloured meadows. High and far
Glistens that ridge above a climber's eyes
When past the canyoned river at his feet,
Circled by tropic vales and verdurous hills,
The vast bulk of the Naked Mountain rears
Blackness of rock and pallor of ice and snow
In tier on tier of glacier and of crag
Through unimagined altitudes. Such height
No eye may see, when swept by the hurricane
The silver plume streams from the yellow rock
Where the broad pyramid of Everest
Seals the Tibetan gorge; or when aloft
Loosens the first faint puff of the avalanche
Spurting white on red cliffs of Kangchenjunga.
Cool are the climber's heights; but first he meets
That sunken chasm, where underneath the hills
Lies like a deep rift in the tawny earth
The huge gorge, with the Indus in its cleft,
Monstrous and turbid with Tibetan snows:
Silent, until some eddy from the depths
Swirls to the surface, blooming as it breaks.
There through the bleached and elemental rock
Bursts the one torrent, and one smooth dell of green
Makes harder the harsh purple and parched brown
Of desert cliffs; throughout the breathless day
Above the traveller's head the naked rocks
Glisten and tremble in the heat, and night
Sultry and windless follows, till at dawn
Some wandering breath, cool from the upper snows,
Brings rest and comfort. Thence the steep way winds

Up by the crumbling scree-slopes, walls of shale,
To the mild uplands where the breezes wander,
Fresh with the firs' breath, and the temperate air
Dallies above the grasses of the meadow,
Ruffling the pools within the glen of flowers,
Where the tall poppy with the golden centre
Sways the blue petals lovelier than a rose's,
Blue for no eye, soft for no hand to touch.
High to the westward spring the buttresses,
Cloaked with their moving ice and fugitive snow,
Where foiled and dead the earliest climber lies;
But east the trail mounts, past the cross of bronze
Reared to the earlier dead by later climbers
For whom in turn the riven glacier waited:
Beyond the last soil, to the shattered ice-field,
The endless imminence of arch and wall:
By fissured snow-fields, fluted towers of ice,
Bright caverns, to the slope that held the tents
Once, when unheard the midnight avalanche
Slid, and for epitaph the searchers laid
The coiled rope and an ice-axe, on the blue
Blocks of smooth ice that hid the smothered camp.
Then through the steepening terraces of snow
Each climber finds those black and shelterless slabs
Where for four winters on the frozen rope
The dead man shook: midway upon the heights,
Where tent by tent sank in the powder-snow,
The black rock single on the glittering slope
Which in his need a climber found, to wait
Through day on day of famine and of blizzard
Until his strength failed: and that further grave
Where shallow snow covers a fallen climber,
Lying in solitude but not in peace
Where on the narrow ridge the frozen spindrift
Tosses from gulf to gulf, and far below
Daylong and nightlong through the mist and storm
Clang the collapsing ice-cliffs. Loftier yet,
The Silver Saddle through the pillared crags
Gives access to smooth slopes, where men have stood
And far to northward traced that mountain-chain
Where the great glacier dominates the peaks
Ranged by its shores, crag by crag, spire by spire

Endlessly reiterated, and summit snows
Nearest to Everest's, yet all in scale
Diminished by that white immensity.
This may the eye see, and the vast convergence
Of Himalayan and Karakoram ranges
Meeting the Afghan summits, to compose
The central snows of Asia; but with blood
Starved in that tenuous air, and labouring lungs
Measuring each stride with pain, the climber's mind
Dully perceives a grandeur of design
Beyond his power to grasp, and exaltation
In apathy or agony expires;
Yet to a loftier height the climbers won
Before the oncoming blizzard, and with hope
Saw that last snow-slope, where the summit keeps
Its shining treacheries for future feet.

This is the mountain-side, and these the men,
Which urged, against my will, passion and thought
From many an easy dream of line and colour
To the harsh violent grandeur of the ice.
Long had I known the visible lovely earth
Like a blind boy receiving his first sight
Before a picture, seeing in the canvas
Orange, and green, and air's bewildering blue,
Mingled in rich confusion—but no form.
Then in the city and the winter woods
Form was revealed, structure to trace and love,
And re-create: such a sculptural clarity
As my verse seeks, when phrase by phrase I mould
The passionate symmetry of line and stanza,
Shaping a poem to simplicity;
And so for long I laboured, of my guilt
Convicted by this mountain: month by month
Creating what I could, not what I must:
Forgetting the true end, content with beauty—
The half-sufficing, the artist's last temptation,
That painless joy which lures him to forgo
The costlier passion of sublimity.

ON A CORNISH
HEADLAND

"Restless? Of course you're restless! Here we are,
Two people, still apart, who should be one,
Whom love, taste, will and judgment all unite,
And still you have not sense to marry me.
Some undiscovered portion of myself—
Two halves of the same country—but in you
All hills and trees and flowers are fairer far,
And all the animals have more grace and colour.
How wasteful is this wait
By two that are but pieces of one whole—
Their love, an instinct that proclaims their union!"
    "So Plato said, or something of the kind:
More mystical, perhaps, but much the same.—
But look down at the turmoil in the bay.
You see that roller rushing to the beach?
Look how an off-shore gale whirls the spray back,
And the sun makes a moving rainbow in it.
What movement everywhere!
The grass cowers, and the sea-thrift in the clump
Shakes pink against the blue, the blue itself
Sets with the whole Atlantic from the west."
    "Why finish with the ocean, as though earth
Were stable, and exempt from restlessness?
Think further, how the mountains of these isles,
Striking south-westward, have their counterparts
Beyond the Atlantic—how Brazilian shores
Could snugly nestle in the Gulf of Guinea—

THE POETRY LIBRARY

As side by side for many an age they lay.
There was a restlessness indeed—the lava
Pouring through fissures, and the new-made coasts
Gaping as both Americas withdrew,
Foot by foot dwindling through the centuries,
Hull down, till all was gone,
And novel and immense foamed the Atlantic.
So mountain-ranges, snapped in half, strayed westward,
Till far in the ancient ocean lands intruded,
Prows crumpling as they moved
In countless folds of Andes and Sierras,
While evermore diverged the broken halves,
Until Columbus sailed
To overtake those far receding shores.
A hundred million years and more—none knows—
That continent required to make the journey
Which in two months or less Columbus made.
How typical of man!
Stupid he may be, and he may be vicious,
But what man does, how quickly it is done!
But you have heard enough
Of shifting seas and wandering continents.
This granite, warm to touch, will last our time,
Any you, my truant continent, are here.
How long must this our separation last,
And why must we move blindly as the lands?
We, while the continents for ever drive
Farther asunder, and the Americas
Drift westward from their European home,
Slide their curve outward from the African gulf—
We two, so long apart,
Can in our union our completion find."

THE WINDFALL

In orchards long ago,
While on the trees, green and unripe,
Fruit beside fruit swung in the wind,
    A single apple sighed:
"Others will grow ripe on the branch,
I shall give way, fail to fulfil
    An apple's destiny."
Out of the west freshened the breeze,
Till from the bough tumbled the fruit
    And rolled to Newton's feet.

★　　★　　★

THE BEECHES

Under the reddening boughs,
As lip from lip withdraws,
Margaret, I watch you stand
And the crisp leaves float by your russet dress,
As once the new leaves damp with April dew
Swept green against your green;
And first of that alternate green and red,
Then of the time to come
I think, when beech-trees take
The starlight on the pallor of their stems,
And show to moon and sun
Curves that renounce at last
All lesser beauty than their nakedness.

MILAN CATHEDRAL
IN STARLIGHT

Seen by a Classical Artist

In the dark square the noises of the night
Voice by voice, wheel by echoing wheel, fall silent,
And undisturbed at last I trace aloft
The soaring of the arches and the columns,
The vast thrust of the flying buttresses,
And high above the circuit of the roof
Those multitudinous marble pinnacles
Glimmering against the stars. And how can thought
Cease with the loftiest spires, the topmost statue
So strangely poised amid the stars of Virgo?
Those lines must be prolonged, the whole Cathedral
Can have no meaning in itself, the stones
Are in their place to lead our thought beyond them.
Thought? Passion, longing, avid to explore
Perspectives dwindling through infinity;
Allured and baffled, through the constellations
Pursuing a frontier that recedes for ever;
Then past the constellations into darkness
Which new light pierces, rays of galaxies
Prolonging the sharp joy, yet foiling it;
Depth swallowed up in height, and height in depth,
Again, and yet again, renewing for ever
Throughout the alternations of that strange
Unending, unbeginning universe,
The exhilaration of the infinite.
Infinite light, infinite mystery:
And all, according to the poet's dream,
Created for one purpose, to allay
That thirst *to know* unquenchable within us:
Allay, not quench. Here, now, if anywhere,
To hold infinity in the palm of the hand—
Infinitude, our being's heart and home—
With something one and indivisible,
The ground and meaning of the universe,

To feel ourselves transcendently at one—
If this is possible, where more than here?
Here do we find the warrant of all dreaming,
Reality reborn within the soul,
The twin infinitudes of time and space
Piercing home with a single barb, and all
That every art strives to convey to man
Communicated in an instant?

                                Absurd!

Is life so narrow, that a single moment
In one perception gives its height, width, depth?
Is man so luckless, that no better quest
Awaits him than the unattainable?
"Set love in order, thou that lovest Me"—
So to the mystic came the voice of God.
And in the happy love of man and woman,
When body and mind meet, fuse, continually,
Then, does not love make many a thing cohere,
Far from each other, and from love remote?
A word completes the earth, and a girl's breast,
Curving, fills all the universe with peace.
Such power for form and order lies in passion.
So in my art one painter uses colour
Defiant of form, and yet Cézanne would make
From the crude colours of a shaggy slope
A landscape built for ever in luminous space.
Control, not absence, of romantic feeling,
Strengthened, not weakened, by the search for form:
Is that not art for me, and life as well?
And in that symmetry what place is there
For the illusion of the infinite?
Or in those skies, to which the stone beguiled me?
There, till the scientists re-change their minds,
Is not infinity abolished, space
Curves ever inward in a shining sphere,
Shot through and through with movement and with light,
The whole taut as a bowstring, not relaxed
Vaguely throughout illimitable space;
And by that perfect orb outmatched, deposed,
Formless infinity allures no more.

Touch but an atom in that universe,
A cosmic constant guides it on its course;
Seek for a law of interstellar space,
Atoms reveal it in a darkened room.
How strangely is this new-discovered world
Balanced and poised, so woven and so curved,
A structure of uncounted subtleties
Forming the vast simplicity of the whole.
Yet is this new? What memory now is stirred?
Yes, such a fabric have I seen and loved,
Far from this Lombard plain, these northern spires,
Bright in the noon of Athens— and may Nature
Have no more mystery than the Parthenon
In August sunlight! First, the Ægean dawn,
When like a Chinese landscape rose the mountains,
Cloud-pedestalled, to shapely peaks of purple—
No one had said their colour made such form,
Nor that the sea runs wine-dark still at sunrise.
Then that last night at sea, and the last dream
When fell-sides glowed with heather, yet I turned,
Reluctantly, to lines of Attic marble.
But on that hill, beneath the Athenian sky
At mid-day, where were the straight, simple lines
I dreamed of? Stylobate, entablature,
Curved upwards, fluted columns with curved sides
Reared intricate patterns of convexities
Toward their invisible meeting-place in air.
What strength could have such grace? Parabolas
Swirled in a delicate rhythm that the eye
Missed, but the dizzying mind and senses knew
Translated into life, joy, power. Yet all
Summed to a simple harmony; the building
Seemed what it ought to be, by being nothing
Of what it seemed. There was no way but that,
Curve with curve subtly interwoven, making
The extreme simplicity that was the whole:
No spires, no infinite, but the consummation
Of that more excellent beauty which resides
In finite things, by passionate minds devised.

TO A CAT IN A
PICTURE GALLERY

A flurry of snow-flakes,
   And out of the street—
Grey paws and grey body—
You came through the doorway
   To sprawl at my feet.

That Umbrian Madonna
   With mantle of blue
By your grey became brighter,
Mantegna's vermilion
   More brilliant for you.

Nuzzling delightedly,
   Cheek, ear and nose
Cold on my warm hand,
Your eyes of soft amber
   With pleasure half-close.

If I see with what rapture
   You stroke your own head
On pretence of caressing me,
Under these paintings
   What more can be said?

Can I doubt that toward Nature
   They followed your plan,
These men who made much of her,
Using her grandeur
   To magnify man?

Clearer the flesh glows.
   Lovelier the face,
For the river that sinuous
Winds, or the shadowland
   Arched in blue space.

For this the brush laboured,
   The mind had delight,
The trees took their colour,
The mountains grew sharper,
   The sky dimmed her light.

How can I laugh at you,
   Cat, as you purr,
With this human to help you
In tickling your ear-roots
   And smoothing your fur?

IN THE SARGASSO SEA
A.D. 1025

[When the Spaniards landed in Mexico, they found an ancient tradition
of a white-skinned, black-bearded man ("Quetzalcoatl" in the native
language) who had come to the land in the distant past and, after
teaching arts and laws to the inhabitants, had set sail on the eastern
ocean with a promise that he would return. Cortes made ruthless use of
this tradition in order to enhance the prestige of the white men he led.

Early in the eleventh century A.D., Icelandic ships sailing from the
newly-colonised coasts of Greenland reached North America, and
explored the coast for an unknown distance to the south.

Christianity was officially, but by no means universally, adopted as
the religion of Iceland in A.D.1000]

> Men that from Iceland
> Have reached these waters,
> Why fear our landfall
>   Or flag at the oars?
> South out of Greenland
> Land has not failed us,
> Coasts that our fathers
>   Named, and new shores—
>
> Markland that tosses
> Its vacant forests;
> Wild grapes of Vineland,
>   The wild corn's green;
> A cape's white sand-dunes,
> And far to southward
> The long sea-beaches
>   No other had seen.
>
> Look, in that weed-bed,
> Out to the starboard,
> A pitcher is floating,
>   Caught in the weed.
> Can land be far off?
> Up with it, show us
> What kind of craftsmen
>   These countries breed.

Seals, and a stopper—
A mouldering parchment—
Runes such as litter
   Byzantine gear.
Bring the Varangian,
Skilled in Greek writings—
Thord, read us the message
   For all to hear.

"Out of the land of gold,
The rich vales and the ruby-laden hills,
Eastward with wind and current ran my bark,
Until the sail fell slack
In the long calm that lies upon this sea,
Whence I shall never gain
My own Ægean birth-land, or return
Back to the western folk
I found and taught and loved.
Not of the gods I spoke
Where gods meant human death,
Pierced hearts uplifted to the sun, from temples
With stonework carved awry,
Lest the presumption of a perfect form
Affront some envious god;
But arts I taught, and laws,
New mastery of the earth,
Not wisdom, but the power,
The leisure and the comfort to be wise.
There shall I not return;
And yet, in time to come,
When from their far-off Mediterranean ports
Ships that I cannot guide
Cast anchor off those shores,
Some may recall the traveller from the East,
And all that Quetzalcoatl did and taught,
Though from that land I sailed
To find death, and this weed-encrusted sea."

Back to the oars there—
Steer to the westward;
Out of the weed-beds
  Press on the course.
Pull, till the prow dips,
Bound for the riches
That wait our taking
  By skill or force.

On, to the Westland.
What if afar off
Dwell, or have perished,
  Gods of the Greek?
Forward, though foreign
Blaze in the night-sky
The Saviour's symbol
  Whom Christians seek.

Far in the Northland
Gods pass in the ice-mists;
Vain in this sun-glare
  To look for Thor;
Nor have Valkyries
Ridden the moon-ways
Over these waters
  To clangour of war.

High in Valhalla
Do you not hear them
Shout to each other
  In envy and shame—
"Look where the heroes
Row to their conquest:
Would we could follow
  And share their fame!"

On, let the foam spin
White from the oar-blades;
Coasts lie before us,
   Rich, unpossessed;
Men to be conquered—
Gods that would shield them—
None upon our side—
   On, to the west.

ON A PATH ON BOW HILL
(SUSSEX)

Back from a vaster scene—
Forests and mountain-chain
Unbroken by the tropics or the Arctic—
Through the dwarfed fields and woods
I come to this low narrow range of downs,
Toy hills the laziest stride
Will cross in half a day,
Following the track I tread:
This greenway that ascends
Above the twisted blackness of the yews
Where random whitebeams flash,
Along the airy shoulder of the down,
To the tall brow above
Where barrow after barrow cuts the sky.
Smooth underfoot the turf,
While thoughts go wandering far
Over that unforgotten western land—
Geography without a history—
Until this circular pit,
Encroaching on the way,
Recalls me to the present, and the past:
To others who have known
This track—some Celt who paused
When Rome was scarce a name,
And Persian fire still spared
The first uncouth ancestral Parthenon;
Paused, as he turned his steps
Round someone's careless hole,
Nor guessed how, fifteen centuries before,
Flint-miners sank their shaft,
Driving the antlered pick
In the soft chalky turf,
To spoil, long since, the path
Smooth for their feet, as for the Celt's and mine.

THE ISLAND

Guess, if you can, the meaning of this dream
Which puzzled me last night, and leaves me wondering.
I'll tell it as it happened, step by step
Re-living it; and if I seem to dwell
Upon the rock, the waters and the mist,
Mere physical externals, you'll remember
I am no preacher of the Word like you,
No mystic restless for an unseen world,
And little I think, in my geology,
Of these deep truths you teach: though recently—
Can it then mean—but you shall judge of that.

I was upon an island: all my life
It seemed that I had lived there, all alone,
Environed by the waters and the mist:
Water that lapped upon the light-grey rock,
Grey ripples, and a grey, perpetual mist
Drifting out of the seas I never glimpsed
To eddy around my sterile promontories.
No childhood I recalled, nor any people—
I needed none; yet folk had been there once
Who built the ruinous castle where I lived;
And there in the old grey walls I stayed content.
That island was my world, and in my dream
I guessed no other, but delightedly
I set myself to knowledge of my home,
Studying the rocks, the sea-coast, and the mist,
But most of all the rock: till one by one
I lit upon such theories as I use
Each day in waking hours, the origins
Of rock shaped in sharp fire, slowly accreting
Under the sea, or born of flowing lava:
And with what joy I made that knowledge mine!
The same, too, with the ripples and the mist;
And often, in a tiny boat I made,
I rowed, far as I dared, out from the island.
Food? In my dream I never thought of that—
You know how I forget it! And so at last
No mystery was left upon that island,
My world was known: What else was there to know?
I had it clear, all clear within my mind,
Save for one point my theories failed to cover:

Why were the waves so small?
On that I pondered, scrambling by the shore
One day upon the tossed, misshapen rocks,
When suddenly I stopped: the mists were lifting!
The grey thinned overhead, and blue came through,
To right and left the mist swirled out of sight,
And there beyond my sea was a new shore,
An unsuspected coast outside the island.
A moment took me to the boat, the oars
Were ready, soon with oars and sail I neared
A strand where wavelets, weak as mine, broke lightly.
Ahead, a cliff; and after that, a hill,
And, as I climbed it, often I looked back
Till I could trace a circuit of brown shores
Which ringed my trivial lake,
And at its heart a fuzz of mist, the island
On which the cloud had settled as before.
A step more, and the crest was mine; beneath me
The land fell at my feet sheer to white sand,
The border of illimitable waves
Rolling bright-blue with windy bright-blue skies
Arching a true, irrefutable ocean.
What force has troughed those waves, gave them their ridges
A mile and more in length? The sands were wet:
Had then the seas withdrawn? Would they return?
What drew them back, what power—and then I woke.
And now what does it mean?
Your pipe's laid down, your eyes smile, do you think—
Ah, yes, I see it now, I think so too.

from
THE
INEFFICIENT
GODS

THE INEFFICIENT GODS

The Second God was by the First addressed:
"Go, scatter the stars, and somewhere find a place,
Sequestered from these precincts, for a test:
From wild, hot, random substance build in space
A world, with fire and water at its base—
Watch well your safety—and to crown the plan
From animal and mud frame a God's face,
Beyond behemoth and leviathan,
That your aeonian work may culminate in Man".

An aeon passed, and once again the Second
Had interview, reporting at a nod:
"Lord, Thy design was perfect, but I reckoned
Too blindly, or the stuff of Man was odd;
The primal beast-mark clings to him, the clod
Remains his fellow — worship has decayed
And gratitude that's owed to every God—
And with fear, pain, desire, his nerves are frayed.
Now shall I extirpate the failure I have made?"

"No—Yes—No—it can hardly matter now,
So drab the world is and so deep the taint.
But Gods must learn by blundering; none would know
Or miss the worship of a world so quaint—
But, taught by failure, model with restraint
A world congenial to us all, a bright
World in that interspace to which I point,
Where the deep double stars across the night
Grow like a bed of flowers, a marvel of violet light."

THE POETRY LIBRARY

THE FIRST PROLETARIAN REVOLUTION
2200 B.C.

The rich are in mourning, the common folk triumphant;
    The towns say, "Let us put down the men of power".
The laundrygirl refuses to carry her burden,
    The doorkeepers say, "Let us go and plunder the house".
The lapis lazuli chain on the slave-girl dangles
    While the rich man's child is dashed against the wall.
Upon their sand-banks the crocodiles lie sated,
    So many rich have gone of their own accord.
And the new rich own the shade, they listen to music;
    She that looked at her face in a pool, in a mirror smiles.
Lo, the Nine Gods open their kingdom to slaves and poor men,
    While the land, like a potter's wheel, turns upside down.

—Abbreviated from the ancient Egyptian

AFTER THE DEFEAT

The Dutch light cruisers 'Java' and 'de Ruyter' were torpedoed
off the coast of Java in February 1942

"From the last combat of a fleet that sank
We come, defeated. First, beyond the seas
Our country fell, and next a crueller foe
Closed on the populous empire that we guarded,
Unarmed if we should fail. One hope there was,
To break the invading convoys. Day by day
We circled through the glittering seas, or fought,
Outmatched by heavier cruisers, till at last,
Crossing the hidden submarine line at night,
We drowned in the hot darkness, far from help,
Nothing achieved; and under the tropic moon
The laden transports, huge and vulnerable,
Sailed on to Java. From that death we come,
The certainty of that defenceless island,
Whose hopelessness embittered all our dying.
But who are you that meet us in this place?"
    "We are the crews of three Athenian ships
Who died as you have died. North of us lay
The Persian navy, anchored row by row
Under Thessalian headlands—to the west,
The tents of Xerxes, and Leonidas
Between the treacherous mountains and the gulf,
Lost if we yielded. Then our squadrons closed,
In hope to shatter the invading fleet
And force that army backward; but by numbers
Beaten, and stubborn fighting of the Persian,
We failed, and galley next to galley sank,
With none to rescue. There our warfare ceased,
And who recalls, out of those years of glory,
At Artemision our obscure repulse?
Our fathers fought at Marathon, our brothers
Broke the invasion that we failed to break,
And our sons reared the Athens all men know,
But we in that achievement took no part.
Yet, though we left no name and won no action,
Not worthless was our combat, since in war
Many must die haphazard, to no purpose,
That other men, on later battlefields,
Equal in skill and courage, may by arms,

Numbers, or luck of battle win the day.
Death we could bear, and death without result,
But not our foresight of the land we left:
Greece disunited, and the separate states
One by one falling victim to the foe;
His fleet, unchallenged, off our plundering coasts,
And monstrous army thronging Attica;
Athens deserted, and her men withdrawn,
To watch in the end the lost Acropolis
Reddening at dusk beyond the firelit straits.
That we foresaw, and on that sight we died.
How could we hope for Salamis, or see
The sub-rays glinting on the Persian shields
Rusting amid the dews of Citheron?"

ADVENTURERS

Lonely, with few or none
To share the perils none had dared before,
The first barbarian drove his coracle
On unbridged Rhine or Rhone,
Or crossed the misty straits
Between French cliffs and islands unexplored.
Small, too, the band
Who thrust the Punic galley past the Rock
Southward to tropic harbours and far seas.
Larger at last the crews
Who made the landfall of new continents,
Slackened the first sails at Pacific isles,
Or perished in the ice-pack; and in war
Mighty at last the fleets that sailed or steamed to battle
When the spars splintered in the cannonade,
Or cordite fume coiled above shattered steel
When under the Jutland billows slid the turreted hulls.

But in the skies tonight
The shells tear at the wings
Where four men drop the bombs on Kiel or Brest;
Over the crimson Thames
Pilot and gunner trail
The bomber that disintegrates and falls;
And over Libyan sands,
As the wan air grows perilous with dawn,
Pilots will search the desert dunes
And dive upon the glinting armoured hulls,
Alone.

AT BATTLE ABBEY ON SEPTEMBER 15th

Foliage of lime and elm
Rustles above the ruins and the gardens
Under the tall grey turrets, while I stand
Where all is changed since that October day
When on this hill the Saxon banner floated
Over rough grass and random-flowering gorse
Behind the spear-heads and the palisades.
Here, as I pause, I learn
How, when the battlefield is cleared, the site
Enters upon its slow vicissitudes,
Deep-furrowed by the plough,
Effaced by forest or by lake, or sealed
Under stone pavements, till that place no more
Commemorates the victory or the dead.
And so I think, beneath the walls and trees,
Of this and many another ground of battle,
Lost, or transformed by nature or by man—
Till from this narrow hill,
These crumbling arches, corridors of box,
The darkness of the cedars and the yews,
I look up to that other battlefield
Past power of man or nature to deface,
To blue sky and white cloud
Where England saved, not lost, her liberty.

HIROSHIMA
The Spirit of Tragedy Speaks

Long have I watched those tragic heroes, doomed
From throne, or court, or Desdemona's arms,
Bewildered to their crisis to be thrust,
Easy for some, hopeless for them to solve;
Each by his own disastrous merits brought
Into that fatal pass, where some one flaw,
Some pulse of passion, some ambitious taint,
Ensures the ruin his best deeds prepared.

And now another meets his crisis: Man,
The adventurous animal, tireless to create,
Who searched for knowledge, and has chanced on power;
While that impartial destiny which gave
Faustus his choice, which showed Macbeth a crown,
Denies him not this power for evermore.

ON T. S. ELIOT and EZRA POUND

"I am never sure that I can call my verse my own;
just when I am most pleased with myself, I find that
I have caught up some echo from a verse of Pound's"
(T. S. Eliot).

Too much you praise him, who so well is known—
Master of every style except his own;
Verses which copy that long mimicry
The echo of an echo needs must be.

ON THE SAME

Long had we known the ape could imitate
    The lion's ramp, and beasts of every shape;
But who had thought to hear the lion state
    It was his turn to imitate the ape?

TWO CONTEMPORARY POETS

(1)

Hard is your toil your master to outrun,
And yet when you have done, we have not Donne,
For at the end in all your work we find
The intricate language, not the intricate mind.

(2)

Originality in every phrase
He's proud to show, and thus himself betrays;
Those who possess it find no need to boast,
While those who have it least esteem it most.

TWO POEMS TO MARGARET

I

As day by day within a poet's mind
Some passionate memory holds its place, and grows
More lyrical and compelling every hour,
Till when the time has come
At last no end is possible but one,
And all those ecstasies of thought and sense
Blent in a poem find their consummation,
Completed in that act:
So, Margaret, in our lives
Week by week deepens and renews our love,
While all we think and do
Urges the mind and body to one end,
The rich fulfilment of these nights and days,
When hovering finger-tips may move our minds
To abstract ecstasy,
Or our thoughts meeting in some airy void
Force hand to hand, lip to lip, breast to breast.

II

Darling, the year may come
When on this breathless hour
We shall look back with insight born of time,
Tracing our love's long course
From this initial day
With wiser lips than these that cling together,
And less desirous eyes.
Then with maturer minds
We may re-live the past
And some philosophy of love compose,
Such as today eludes
These lips, these hands, these eyes,
Heedless of all beyond love's ecstasy.

KISS

"Before we met,
What had you found nearest to this?"
"Why, this above all: times when the blind
Power that creates fused into one
Passion and thought,
To meet in my verse there, as they meet
Here in a kiss, Margaret — but poems
Never kiss back!"

STORM OVER CORNWALL

The wing-tip takes the cloud, the cloud the wing,
And the hull lurches as the wild grey smother
Left and right flings her, down and up. Below,
A moment since, the green and white Atlantic
Heaved, hazardous and restless for the ships.
Now—the cloud breaks, a wreck with slanting bows
Turns all the running green to angry foam.
Again the momentary grey, then shreds
Of flying cloud let through a violent glimpse
Of the whole ocean thwarted and uprearing
On Land's End and its granite, white, unheard.
A black cloud waits us, half the wing is hidden,
Hail flogs the hull, drives level past the window,
The plane tilts; and again the storm is past,
Level and smooth we ride beneath the sun,
Green pastures and the long brown moors below,
White with a single cloud—what's that upon it?
Purple and green and orange form a ring,
A moving ring, a rainbow in a circle,
Sliding along the surface of the cloud,
And in the ring the shadow of the plane,
Hull, engines, wings and tail distinct and black,
Black wing-tips folded close by glowing purple.
How fast it follows us! Now it is gone—
The cloud is lost behind us.
What more than this could man ask, seek what symbol
Better than this, of life and what life holds?
Colour throughout its range, consummate form,
Swift movement, and at heart of all a shadow.

ON A LAKE IN NEW ENGLAND

"Now in the far-off English scene
    The scentless, songless months are gone,
October brings again the green
    Blended with russets of her own."

"Better this lake on which we drift,
    Better—in depths beneath our keel—
The crimson boughs that lightly lift
    That yellow oriole to reveal.

"Better this flare of forest leaves
    Than all the Asian hues and spice,
When fruit and blossom both were Eve's
    In her fantastic paradise."

"Brief is the brilliance that you praise;
    Yet, till the final wintry squall,
Enjoy your maples while they blaze,
    Your Paradise ending with the Fall."

CONSCIENCE

"I am the moral law.
I speak to you, an artist,
Saying, as I say to every man:
Be unselfish."
"Great and unquestioned your authority,
And in my breast
Still turns your sharp three-cornered instrument
Which blunts if long ignored.
And yet a second voice,
Insistently, austerely as your own,
Calls, saying:—
'When will the work be finished,
Your eight years' labour?
Recall the sterile years
When each impression craved, but lacked, expression;
Recall that earlier time
When all was false, or vague, or new;
Then, later years recall
When the long shame of barren receptivity
Was half redeemed in verse,
Brief, with no synthesis,
Marginal notes to one unwritten poem.
Now the design's complete,
Now the words come which fled from you so long:
All past experience and all partial verse,
Love, gratitude, and instinct bid you hasten:
And still, how long?'
So urges, nay commands, that other voice.
Must you command no less?"
"I speak as the moral law,
Abating nothing,
And though obedience to my utmost word
Leave your life's-work undone,
That is no charge of mine.
Solve as you may your problem,
Still I shall speak, and you must listen still."

FIRST EVENING IN EGYPT

Under a palm-tree
Canopus
Shines above the desert-sand.

In England,
Even in Italy and Greece,
These three were symbols, three unattainables.

Am I glad or sorry,
Finding tonight
This silent death of so much longing?

HAWTHORN

A day or two ago,
Lingering in this deep lane beneath the young
White of the may, that's still so far from must,
I might have felt that sharp familiar impulse
Stirring to phrases, a poem, about these petals.
Now, numb and tired, watching with mind and sense
Aloof from all their beauty,
Impotent to create, or even enjoy,
I muse, impatient with the blossoming may
Because it cannot wake that deep delight
Which finds fruition only in a poem:
Till in this barren mind
The savage consciousness of impotence,
Rousing more passion than enjoyment could,
Begets this verse.

ON A PATH IN AFRICA
The Host to the Poet

"Turn the bend and pass the tree;
   Put the straggling creepers by;
   Catch the sudden glimpse on high
   Of the blue flower of the sky;
      Then beyond the rotting log,
Red with ants, turn left and see—
      By that green bewildered frog—
The strange jumble on the track:
   Sticks exposed to every weather,
   Loosely laid in a heap together,
Green and sappy, damp and black—
   How could such sticks make a fire?
      Who could fancy they would blaze?"
"Drunken tribesmen?"
         "Never! Beer
Breeds a different desire.
      Yet it's true the African lays
Fire-heaps that are copied here;
   And the arms were black that laboured.
   Chimpanzees that long have neighboured
Tribesmen in this Cameroon
   Sometimes watch unseen, while late
      Parties gather sticks to burn;
So they see the camp-fire strewn,
      Watch the flames the tinder swallow,
Light and heat emerge together—
      Then, they say, the apes in turn,
Grinning, clumsy, grope and gather
   Sticks like these, and hunched-up wait
      Eager for the flame to follow."

The Poet To Himself

Eager, indeed, for any flame to come:
They followed the approved routine, then wait
Hopefully, but for what? For what must come
Otherwise — that is obvious — but for me
Not obvious, in the havoc of a life
Which, I now see, a foiled ape typifies.
What made him bring me to this place, and tell
This story that's a symbol of myself?—
An ape hand gathering sticks; mind, life, all aimless.
Once there was aim, when all was geared to poetry
Which justified my living; every habit
Serving that work, selfishness otherwise.
Nothing of all is left
Now, but each habit, tedious to myself,
Far worse for others: unenkindled sticks
Which of themselves can give no light, know nothing
Of the live coal which from the hallowed altar,
Grave-faced, the seraphs bore to living lips,
Making the seared lips utter — the harsh fire,
Inhuman, inextinguishable, whose touch
Isaiah—Pushkin—craved for prophets, Milton for poets.
   No hope is here: only a far-off glimpse—
There—of his "blue flower in the sky", where burn
Beyond our intermediate sunless world
Vast firmaments that African lightnings pierce;
Or the aircraft drifts above her drifting shadow
Down pavements of the sunbright cumulus
To the sudden rift — the forest's sunward side
Where the looped purple blossoms dazzle at the sun.

A HILL IN THE SOUTH

I climb a hill,
In day-dreams and in night-dreams climb a hill
Where the soft wind and clarity of light
Make England turbid, Italy confused,
And the warm lucid air embracing olives
Amid the craggy limestone's light-grey ledges
Blows from no Apennine or Pennine height—
What is it but Aegean? So it was,
When year by year Hymettos was the hill,
Athens the city; for I craved the Greek,
The bounded, the efficient, and the luminous.

Now, two hills rise
Recurrently with olives and with limestone—
Each with enchantment of Dantean light
Purging the will, feeding the mind with love.
Which hill is it to-day? Now if I turn
Upon Hymettos, or on Olivet,
And face the sunset, shall I see the cone
Of Lykabettos, and the Acropolis
With fluted columns intercepting light—
Or harsh grey ramparts of Jerusalem?
—There is the place where Godfrey stormed the wall,
Then the blood poured through mosque and synagogue;
Gehenna there; there, perhaps, Golgotha;
Beyond the Kedron vale—an Arab's plan,
Greek-built (the Parthenon's equal?) —there, the Dome of the Rock:
That blue dome brilliant with the Saracen titles
Which canopies the rough primaeval rock,
Moriah's rock, too sacred for a pavement,
Where rose Mohammed into heaven, beginning
That long plot-sequence which in Dante ended—
Where Christ's foot stepped—where Solomon built his temple—
Where David stood to watch
The chaff dispersing on the threshing-floor—
Where Abraham found the ram, and Isaac lived:
That bare rock still, below the wealth of the world.
Close by, El Aksa Mosque where King Abdullah
This year died, murdered in his holy place.
How to escape (ever again escape?)
That fantasy of overshadowing wings
Dripping slow gouts upon this city of blood?

I climb a hill
Once more, eager to glimpse beyond the ridge
Pellucid bays, and a white crown on Sunion;
But the scene flickers, and the limestone crest
Plunges to that Judaean Wilderness
Where the bare earth is monstrous, and each path
From blanched sterility to blanched sterility
Leads, and no devil's needed to tempt man
To desperate thoughts. Where Greece may reconcile,
And all things work within you to a centre,
Here's violence and disruption and despair—
Things tearing apart that tear you in their tearing—
Saying "Renounce" where Athens says "Fulfil"—
And yet . . . may a part exceed the all of Athens?

Sunset upon a hill,
And a voice speaking from a earlier sunset,
There where the brook bends at Aceldema:—
"On the third day, on the third day he rises.
I found him true in one unflinched-at kiss,
Still true beneath the shouts, the blows, the nails,
Faithful in every word, no promise void.
The second sun sets there behind the Temple,
And with to-morrow's dawn . . .
Doubt and bewilderment consume the others—
I killed him—I see clearly—I believe.
How could I meet his risen eyes to-morrow,
Be touched by the torn hand, escape those feet
Less hindered by their wounds than birds by wings?
Mine also is a tree, mine this rough rope."
Now it is night,
And the olives speak of peace, and peace, and peace.
Which now? Jerusalem? Athens?—A cock crows.

WHO CAN HIDE A RAINBOW?

In England (1955)
"So far, no land has satisfied you fully:
What are your specifications?" So I brooded:-
"First, a mountain-range, and I'd define
'Mountain' as something that has glaciers on it.
A desert, next; then forests, and for choice
A tropical jungle; one of the world's great rivers;
A sea-coast, and an ocean; one thing more—
Monuments of an ancient civilization."
"But where?—even if you took your cue from Johnson:
'Let Observation with extensive View
Survey Mankind from China to Peru'."
"A trifle clumsy?—This is what he's saying:—
'Let observation with extensive observation
Observe mankind from China to —' that's it!
Why, I described Peru."

Beyond Cuzco (1969)
The coastal desert's far behind, and the train,
In this, earth's lengthiest mountain-range, turns downwards
From thirteen thousand feet,
Hairpinning to the Urubamba canyon . . .
And now this jungle of the Amazon
Adjoins our track; by buttress-rooted trees
White orchids invite the tiny humming-birds
To fly in, and then backwards out; wild dahlias,
Begonias, fuchsias, thickets of nameless yellow,
Border the white-flecked brown of the waters, where
Clenched in its more-than Himalayan gorge
The Urubamba raves; toss a stick—
Four thousand miles away the Atlantic waits.
Vertical, green and black,
Soar the incessant cliffs—at a bend, a snowpeak
Glitters at twenty thousand feet; still higher,
Andean cumuli
Drift, the most perfect cloudscapes of the world.

What's addable to this gorge? The most spectacular
Of archaeological sites, New World or Old?

The train stops. Two thousand cloudy feet above us
A narrow isthmus joins two conical peaks,
Machu and Huayna; on that steep saddle lies
The Inca city the Spaniards never found.
A quaint road spirals up. To sculpt the peninsula
The Urubamba enfolds the cliffs of Huayna.

Night in Machu Picchu

The granite glitters softly in the moonlight,
This smoothly curving ashlar I put my hand on.
Discernible, the colours of wild blue lupin
And tall red canna lilies. Snakes?—perhaps, none.
All's still intact—only the thatch has gone —
The houses wait their folk, temples their worshippers,
In this serene Pompeii of the clouds.
Gorge-wards, the stone-banked terraces where grew the maize.
Two llamas—milky in the moon; and there
People with torches—no! too quickly
The soft lights dart—fireflies that dance in the temple.
Both right and left, the thunder of the river.

THE POETRY LIBRARY

Machu Picchu by Day

Day: summer, and the rainy season;
Sideways at every angle lean the flowers,
Grey walls behind them, a smooth green plaza,
And past the floating mists the high-tiered peaks,
Midsummer snow above that tropical torrent.
— Curved stones, like the timple of the Sun in Cuzco:
When the Andes shrugged their shoulders, the christian church
Collapased, the Inca temple re-emerged.
here, in this perfect architecture, how easy
To people again this town with Indian faces!
One moment quicker, and up that stair you'd see
an Inca's robe, his ankle, vanishing.
— Alpaca lambs — how pink their inner ears!
Their mothers spit half-heartedly, as I crawl
Up Inca steps for a worm's eye view of llamas.
Rain, and I shelter; then the brilliant sun —
There must be a rainbow. (Did the Inca girls,
Shaking their two black braids, call, "See the rainbow"?
Confidently I turn, and search the sky.
None, but there must be! — who can hide a rainbow?
Obstinate, I round the temple, cross the saddle:-
Hundreds of feet below me, spanning the gorge's
dark cliffs and the Urubamba's savage brown,
Arc all the colours.

In Mexico,
I learnt the way of the new community,
The schools, revived traditions — Nahua, Maya —
Land redistributed; but in Peru, unaltered,
Indians prolong exploited centuries:
Scarce land; no Quechua schools; no care for the people.
— yet in Peru, with these new drastic rulers —
Despite the padlocked gate of Parliament,
That sentry inside it fingering his rifle —
Is the hidden rainbow waiting to be found?

NO ONE PAINTS FUJI
Shiba Kokan, 1765

At last: I will take this slowly—
I part these flowering cherries, left and right;
The lake's bright at my feet; before my toes
The water holds a sharp white cone, which widens,
Still white, further away upon the pond;
Then white gives way to broader browns and greens,
Spreading across the lake in flawless symmetry;
Fuji's cone, inverted; and then that bank
Where a wagon passes slowly, reflected in the water:
Beyond, deep-snowed aloft in the sun of spring,
Our sacredest mountain's true and upright cone.

Yet no one paints it!

With China as our model, textbooks tell us
How to draw hills—prescribe the number of strokes
For the figure of a traveller on a bridge:
But there's a gap, for China has no fire-peak.
So men shrug barrenly at Fuji,
Lost for a model, adrift for precedents—
Draw a mist-wreathed slope, claim "I paint the spirit
Of Fuji"—dishonouring, disuniquing her.
But I, too lack a method.
Fuji, my Fuji, loved so desperately,
Must I die failing you?

UNDER THE NORTH FACE OF THE MATTERHORN
(First climbed by Franz and Toni Schmid in 1931)

Spreadeagled on the sheer
Slope of that jutting crag,
Midway upon those cliffs which none had climbed,
With ropes lashed to the nails
Hammered in creviced rock,
Throughout a frost-bound night
The brothers waited till the dawn was near,
Then loosed the icy knots,
To crawl some steep and perilous yards
Before the cliff at sunrise volleyed stone and ice.

Down in the Zermatt vale
The autumn crocus snapped
As the ripe pastures fell before the scythe.
Not on that mountain-wall,
Or hard-won summit-ridge,
Might climbers leave behind
The transience of autumnal fields and woods:
Ceaseless the hail of rock
Discharged upon each granite flank
While year by year the ruinous peak disintegrates.

Yet in the secret depths
Where earth sways like the sea
The forces have not ceased that built the Alps.
Watching the fissured rocks
Loosen and fall apart,
How should men think to trace,
Beneath the vast curve of the mountain-chain,
Some subterranean force
Which, as the separate crags decay,
Heaves vale and ridge and snowfield nearer to the sun?

CHINA IN SPRING

"It's only when you see their country in spring that you begin to understand why the English have written the best goddam poetry in the world"
(Harry Hopkins, Roosevelt's personal envoy, in April, 1942)

And China too,
The southern China of the monsoon rains,
Till the cloud-muffled dawn is briefly dry
And the tall trees march with their deep pink blossoms
Around the margins of that lake which spreads
Widening, fading into the mist-filled distance
Or paths at Shaoshan where the small boy ran
Between the two ponds, desperate
When he would drown himself that night
If his father beat him again—not fear but anger
(The two small ponds with smiling neat schoolchildren
Walking beyond them to Chairman Mao's first home);
And everywhere in the woods the rough-barked trees
Dangling their great white flowers with golden centres;
The interminable purple of a sunlit
Crop on the valley-floor, and set against it
The geometric brilliance of young rice
Green in wet plots, between azaleas' crimson
And the blue mountain-cone, that peak of Shaoshan.
Are there still leopards in those forested mountains
Where Mao scrambled, a bitter line in his head:
"If Heaven had feelings, Heaven too would become aged."?
In the end, six thousand miles
Were not too long a march, and Marxist doctrines
Turns that old Chinese loser—a peasant rebellion—to success.

Kweilin at dusk,
When the sad-coloured twilight makes one monotone
Of flooded rice-fields, daggering the shadows
Of scores—I count them, hundreds—
Of separate mountainous pinnacles of limestone,
"Like green jade hairpins";
All's flat and wet, or vertical and parched;
Improbable
Beyond the improbable shapes of Chinese paintings.
—Kweilin at night, and the soft friendly clapping
From boys and girls, unseen, as we pass their lane.

In Peking "there's no spring", the guide-book says.
None? Not our Western blossoms, but a season
Grander, unparalleled,
As though the vast flare of autumn leaves were
Transposed to brilliantest green;
The willows of Peking, new-planted in their myriads.
White and pink plum and peach
Foam round the Ming pavilions, crimson-pillared;
And round the Wall
Where no flowers grow in the harsh mountain grass,
The wild white blossoming plums
Climb up the sullen slopes,
One of "three friends that do not fear the cold";
While westward towards the Gobi—"To break the sandstorms
We're planting a belt of trees,
A mile wide, and a thousand miles in length".

Before I saw this land in April,
I'd say: "Whatever its realistic base,
The Chinese had the greatest landscape painting;
And, until modern times, say, eighty per cent
Of the best nature poetry was theirs."
I never thought I'd ask: "To China, did even
Her painters do full justice? And her poets?"

UNKNOWN TREES IN NEPAL

In Pókhara

I came to see the mountains, not the trees.
— That aircraft-captain, pointing: "The dark mountain,
The one without snow's Everest; you're looking at
The south-west face. This morning you are lucky:
Eight out of ten of the world's highest peaks;
Three to four hundred miles". And there they lay,
The central Himalayas in their gentle curve,
Arced like a bent bow to the left and right,
Covered with new snow in the winter sun,
And not a cloud, except the summit-banners.
That I had flown to see . . . and here in Pókhara
That lake, the wild poinsettias' scarlet blaze
And those sheer precipices, so near, of Annapurna.
All *that* I had come to find; why should I trouble
Now with these unknown trees,
Bordering my grassy path downhill to the airstrip,
Each on its spacious platform built of stones?
— A beech, at first far glimpse, with that smooth bark —
But vaster far the bole, taller the tree,
Wider the outward thrust of huger branches.
On slender stems, great heart-shaped leaves are poised.
What are they? How famous, if in Europe, but
In central Nepal, there's none to know or praise them!

In Kathmandu

"Those trees"—and I described them—"what were they?"
"Peepuls, or bo-trees; did you not observe
That shade they cast? Your prophet Elijah,
Despairing in his desert, had no shade
But juniper, so wished—as well he might—for death.

But our Lord Buddha, all his fasting over,
Disowned by his disciples, found a peepul-tree
And quietly sitting, with no God to help him,
Achieved Enlightenment, became "the Buddha';
"Bodhi-" or "Bo-tree" means the "the tree of light".
(That first tree's dead, but its authentic child
Stands aged in Ceylon, its grandchild in Banaras).
You know he was Nepalese — how great a gift
For so small a country to offer all mankind!
And everywhere, linked with the Buddha's teaching—
The peepul-tree, remembered in all the arts
Throughout the populous lands of southern and eastern Asia,
Twenty-five centuries, and still today.
That tree has meant more to more folk than any other".

So I, ashamed, was
Trapped in my narrow Western-centredness;
Because I did not know, thought that none knew;
And treated with a kind of ignorant pity
This, the most famous tree of all.

THE
WAY
IN
THE
JUNGLE

THE WAY IN THE JUNGLE

On the last night before the western rains
Flooded the jungle, I listened in a hut,
Entranced, appalled, to the noises of the night.
'Tigers?' I asked, 'or leopards?' But my host
Shrugged, spread his hands, and smiled: 'Frogs, mostly.' 'Frogs!'
'Frogs are important, and our Vedic hymns
Are courteous to them; there's a wedding song—
      Man longs for woman, as naturally
        As the parched frogs long for the rain.'
'As naturally, but not as noisily!'
     The rains fell, and I mused upon Micaiah—
Always, 'The Lord has spoken', not 'Let us see',
No humble, fumbling train of reasoned thought;
And no art. If, in some simpler world,
If beauty, grandeur, sprang from good alone,
Were truth found only by the virtuous man,
Or goodness reached but by the way of truth!—
But life has many ends, and means to each,
And the slaves' blood beneath Assyrian towers
Blurs not the colours, warps no line or curve:
All's clean and pure as if clean hands had reared it.
Anthea's words recurred:-
      By this we know that they are Gods, not men,
      That their hearts break not with our misery.
      In such a unvierse how think to find
      A pitying heart, or unmacabre mind?
'No art'. And yet . . . in the end . . . I seemed to hear
The thin, sharp voice of Phoenix, speaking words
Like these:- 'Though this man has no care for art,
Others will care. That passion of belief
Must issue in the end in stone, paint, music:
Since, when all hearts are stirred, the hands of someone
Will have no rest until the paint is dry,
A lyre sounds, or a building takes the sun.
How can the heart within
Give worship, and the hands and tongue do nothing?'

Some future painter, with divided mind,
A sense of sin, a conflict in himself,
In prayer and despair before an olive-wood?—
                'Will the blue float me nearer to his heaven,
                Or if I catch the gnarl of the olive-trees,
                Will that avail for cleansing, or annul
                The barrier that excludes me from my God?'
It could be so; what new forms, then, of art?
        The rains, so unbelievable, ended at last,
And I turned eastward,
A moving meal for ticks, mosquitoes, leeches,
Beneath the great trunks with their buttress roots,
The flowering flame-trees, and the peepul trees
That left our beeches tiny. At first, alone;
But then along the winding forest-tracks,
Among the herdsmen and the villagers,
I met with wandering men, alone or in bands,
Naked, emaciated, who brooded on Gods—
Familiar names, Varuna, Dyaus, but others
New to me, Agni, Vishnu, Indra most of all.
I had learnt their language—akin to mine—but not their thoughts.
Powerful, capricious, bawdy—
Such were the Gods of my own land, whom Phoenix
Had seen with new eyes; but in Indra's land
Subservience and contempt, deep reverence and
Total rejection, all were possible attitudes—
But not Micaiah's one God with a purpose
For one race to fulfil his covenant.
        And then I met Mahindo,
Fair skinned, with eyes that smiled when the mouth smiled,
Speaking the northern language. A prince's son,
He taught still with the habit of command.
        'Whom do you teach,' I asked, 'priests, princes—whom?'
        He shook his head: 'We are all adrift, we men,
Upon one raft on the ocean of life's troubles.
I speak to all, I choose my words for all,
Simplest for simple men; kings listen least.'
        'Women?'
        'A few.—I could not have prevailed, had the body
Contained a second impulse, strong as sex.'
        'How did you learn?'
        He chuckled: 'Slow—slower—slowest when I fasted

Month upon month, until my ribs stood out
Like beams of an old shed, and when I rubbed
My stomach I felt my spine below my fingers.
—All useless; that was not my Way, which is
A Way of discipline but not extremes;
A Way of thinking too.'
      'What God', I asked, 'taught you this Way you've found?'
      'None; Gods are not teachers; I count myself
Teacher of men and Gods; they, too, these Gods—
Indra, a former and a future man—
Seek to escape re-birth, escape as men. Expect
Nothing from pitiless Gods penned in their own despairs—
All from yourself.'
                'But surely this world of ours
Was by some God created?'
                        'No! The truth
Is subtler: our universe—or multiverse—
Was by no Gods created; later they came,
And some power knows, or maybe does not know,
What happened in the pre-God days, pre-man.'
      'You worship, then, no Gods?'
                    He shrugged: 'The Gods
Are dead, or alive, it matters not; man grows,
And man has duties. No God could change to defeat
The victory of a man over himself:
A man with senses quiet as the well-trained horses
Of some great charioteer.—But we must share;
I am not one of those who say:
          "Like the lion not trembling at noises,
            Like the wind not caught in a net,
         Like the lotus not stained by water,
            I shall go wandering alone
               Like a rhinoceros."
      'You learnt this as a youth?'
'No, I was married: that last night — Napara,
The moonlight on the oval of her face
As she slept—'I stared at him: 'You left your wife?'
'Others have given up all; none, her; nothing
But the whole world's long pain beseeching me—

THE POETRY LIBRARY

So much I loved her.' I looked at him, believed him.
    'In Colchis,' I said, 'where died my friends, my wife,
In Colchis when no hope remained, all life
Seemed to me tragedy.'
        'Your western word; my word is "suffering".
    'You act —'
                        'Why, out of pity for the world
Whose suffering I must share. I'd be a lamp
For those in need of a lamp, a willing slave
To any who need a slave, a bridge for men
Seeking the further shore; and when I suffer
Let me be glad of such a suffering, that
Helps, slightly, to release the world from suffering.'
    'What is the Way you teach?'
                        'The Way is in us.
Each man must draw himself out of his mire
As elephants pull themselves out of mud;
And by no flight in the air can a man escape
The suffering that must follow a selfish deed.
Hatred will never cease by hating, but only
By our not hating: anger is overcome
By absence of anger; evil, by doing good;
Greed, by a liberal hand; lies, by the truth.'
    'You spoke of birth, re-birth, life upon life—
You call that inescapable?'
                        'Not quite.
All is as slow as if a tiny bird
Touches with a leaf once in a hundred years
A Himalayan peak, to wear it away.
But at the very end
The good man nears the prize of no re-birth,
And one will grasp it; but for my own part —
No! What I gain I give to others.'
                        'How?'
    He paused: 'An age ago, there lived a king
Rich in gold, grain and chariots. He had three sons,
Young princes, who walking in a park one day
Heard a low moaning in a bamboo thicket,
Deep in a pit: a tigress, with five cubs

A few days old: birth, hunger, pain, all racked her,
Too weak to move and hunt, and the cubs, milkless,
Must die too; two of the princes spoke in pity,
Drawing comparisons and morals, but the third
Silent, threw himself down within her reach
That she might eat, and live, and her cubs live . . .
I was that prince.
But I have far to go; this present life
Is not my last, nor do I see all clearly.
Perhaps in my next . . .'
    'That story,' I said; 'your feeling was of love?'
He nodded: 'The word will serve, though some love's worthless—
Love like a pink smell floating in the air—
For even love's no substitute for thought,
Nor for self-mastery.'
    We parted, and I took my eastward way.
How strange! Then rose my questions:- 'Just suppose,'
'What if?' and 'Could it be . . . ?' But like an echo
I seemed to hear him: 'Your question is not rightly put.
Not memory but forgettery you need;
You must re-think.' How Lindia would have liked him!
—I could hear her: 'So wary you are of women! Try
Reversing your sequence—women, then Gods, then men.'
    Mahindo and his successors: should they prevail,
What pity-grounded arts, caste-free society,
When some great king, listening at last, repays
The debt he owes to every living creature.
    Months later, a broadening river flowed to the east;
And there I asked myself: Had those great cities
Perished for nothing? I recalled Mahindo,
Expounding karma, which transmits
From one birth to another the fruits of actions.
'Micaiah,' I'd said, 'had heard a story of
A snake in a garden, tempting a man and woman,
Whence sin entered the world, and binds the human race.'
'Yes, karma! We have a proverb here: "The fox
Knows of a hundred tricks, the hedgehog one,
But a big one"; your Hebrews know one karma,
But a big one.' 'You learnt this from the dark-skinned people

In the wrecked cities?' 'Karma, yoga, Shiva—
They taught us much, and yet in the end prevailed
Varna, or colour—theirs was the lowest caste.'
        A coast, at last, facing an eastern ocean.
The moon was full; the wind blew to the east;
A falling star shot eastward; in a bay
Was moored a boat with two outriggers, pointing
Like a bronze arrow-head into the east.
Then, dawn; I waited, and—
Called out, as a green flash blazed at my eyes
From the first fragment of the rising disk.
A sign? At least an invitation!
I thought of earlier failures—
The great volcano unclimbed, Colchis returned to;
This time I would go on.
        — I am close to the end of my story—In a boat
Trading for tin, I crossed that eastern sea,
And then, in fishermen's outrigger boats,
Curious but safe, I worked my eastward way,
Month after month, past island after island—
The green volcanic summits, plume-surmounted,
Peering above the dazzling limestone cliffs.
Great trees there were, and an enigmatic proverb—
'If the trees grew too tall, the rats would eat the stars.'
        No skills, no cities—but on boat or raft
One famished man had drifted here, westward across an ocean.
—Backward, to him, these islands! In his land
Heraldic loomed and smoked three white volcanoes
While black in the coloured jungle stood the huge
And thick-lipped bodiless heads of basalt, smiling.
No sculpture here—but new were our wheels, bronze, animals.
        Strange foods they gave me, spices unknown to us,
Worth a long journey, so it seemed I moved
Forward in space, and forward too in time—
A part of the future, when men brown and white
Would sail, with winds assured, upon these seas,
Where blows a wind from the west, which must be wet,
And after it a dry wind from the east.
The western wind blew hard, until at last
Alone in a scudding boat I reached this place."

DESERT
DEATH

DESERT DEATH

(Seleucos the Astronomer, 150 B.C.)

Now what remains of Zeuxis save his boast,
"My paintings make me immortal"? There they crumble,
There in deep Hellas, where the visiting rain
Forgets few months—unlike this place of death
Where the hard blue of desert mountains closes
The blind white waste of salt Iranian flats:
Blue and white, of a brilliance strange to Zeuxis,
For my last sight beyond the cave's brown ledge.
Yet there is water still, a little food,
And flesh that pains too little to destroy
Thinking, the joy and essence of my life,
Now mixed with sharper feeling, as the end
Makes all except one question obsolete:
Will men remember? Or will heads shake, lips smile:—
"Seleucos? Born on Tigris, young he fell
Under the influence of Hellenic thought—
Forgot, perhaps, his Babylonian teachers—
Then, as a man, framed theories of the tides,
With stranger heresies we leave in silence.
He died in exile in the eastern wastes."—
Is such my epitaph?

    Of the tides I need not think—they were not central
In thought of mine; yet there was little Greek
In those long hours by the Erythraean Sea,
Watching, and timing—timing, too, the moon
From phase to phase, strange ruler of the tides.
But there the common thought was right, the moon
Goes round the Earth, she is but what she seems,
Of little interest: but that setting sun—
"Let us suppose", so Aristarchos said,
"That Earth rotates—revolves around the sun".
His the guess, mine the proof.
But for reward I heard the cry: "This fellow
Defiles the holy heart of the universe;
Indict him, lest for this man's sin his kinsfolk
Endure the vengeance of the insulted Gods."
"Insulted Gods"!—it was their own discomfort—
The bedclothes of their cosy tucked-in world
Torn from their ears, chill winds from outer space

Startling them, when they found their placid Earth
Tossed sidelong into space, to spin in the void
Amid the homelessness of—no, the glory
Of faintly guessed-at new infinity:
How else to explain the stars, so immobile
Viewed from extremities of Earth's wide orbit?
        They said to me: "If Earth rotates, a body
Falling, should fall out of the vertical."
Yes: if men dug a pit
Deep to Earth's centre, and let fall a stone,
The stone would strike the shaft on the eastern side—
Or so I argue; but we have no pit.
        Arguments! Arguments! A dying man
May spare himself, and end in contemplation.
Another Zeuxis? No, my work may lapse,
All manuscripts be lost, all men conspire
To purge their soiled lips of impiety
By never uttering Seleucos' name
Or his discoveries—but they cannot check
The revolution that for evermore
Is vibrant in the uttermost universe;
And when no reader of my book is left
The sun's gilt text and marginal Earth and stars
Must claim new readers of their own, unmoved
By heresy-mongering fools.
        Here with this sand I build a cone, then slice it
So, with my dagger, sideways — now the plane
Shows an ellipse for outline; what's ignoble
In such a shape? Why must a universe
Be built of circles? — Yes the Greeks think thus.—
Draw a chalk line straight on the ground, hold low
A hen's beak to the line, thus push the hen
Over it—soon the bird's bemused—no less
The Greeks with circles in their universe.
Now in the crumbling sand
Again, and for the last time, I will draw
The ellipses of the orbits of the planets:
Here, Hermes—Aphrodite—and the Earth—
Ah, what a symbol of man's life, his planet
Here in her orbit, evermore beset
By Aphrodite there, and Ares here!

Hybrid and mongrel that I am, I share
The hybridness of Him (or Them) that framed
This world so baffling to pure Greeks, pure Arabs.
For, to confound the Greeks, the Eternal Author
Smiles, tossing dice, and bids his globes revolve
In varied orbits round the anchored sun:
And what may tempt him of parabolas,
Deft tangents, loose and spiral shapes, who knows?
Yes, simpler than my masters of Chaldaea
(Too prone to their complexities of Gods)
But subtler than the geometric Greeks,
Half Greek, half Arab, is the Lord of All.

   The sun sinks low above that western peak.
I should be grateful for those old disputes,
Forgetting, as I have, the dwindling food,
And this so thin, so brittle ankle, that
Destroyed, past hope of rescue, all my life:
Of hunger, not of thirst, may my death come!
I have heard there is little pain.

         No, not a Zeuxis, whose paintings flake in ruin.
We share our secret, Earth and sun and I—
No fourth.
Yet with what weakness I desire, surmise—
What centuries away?—a vindicator:
One who will say, "I had one predecessor;
Aristarchos guessed, but Seleucos knew"—
Then back he'll turn with joy
To trace the subtle whirling symmetries.
—I scare dare hope it.—Yet these bones shall rot
Within no cranny of a stagnant world
But share the dignity of Earth's great motion,
The swift diurnal spin against the east
And orbital revolution year by year.

A TRAVELLER
FROM
STRATFORD
1608

A TRAVELLER FROM STRATFORD
1608

A library in Florence; manuscripts,
With many a drawing by da Vinci's hand,
Scattered along the tables; an old man,
Showing the treasures of his deepest shelves
To a single visitor new-come from England,
Whose face is Shakespeare's; yet not the man we know
Who wrote of Antony, Othello, Lear,
And quiet in Stratford died; but in his place
A man diminished by a task declined—
That man who would have been, that lesser man,
Had will, not genius, failed and left undone,
After his comedies of discord, the tragedies.
"You see, sir, how he wrote: from right to left,
With the left hand; easy for him to read,
With practice from a schoolboy; but for others
Impossible, until you use a mirror—
Now you can read it. 'As a day well spent
Brings tranquil sleep,' he writes, 'so life well used
Earns us a tranquil death.' And yet he died
Saddest of men, as mortal sinners die,
Past comforting, all for no sin but this,
That he had failed in labouring at his art:
He, to whom earth has bred no equal yet
Through all the arts! Yet to what vain pursuits
Long years were given! Who may compute the hours
He spent upon the codex I transcribed,
Which yesterday you studied; or count the sheets
In these disordered folios from Milan
Like this sheet, where he charts a vein, then likens
The flowing of the blood within the body
To water drawn from the ocean, travelling far
In a great circuit, mountain, stream, and sea,
Impelled in constant motion. Then below,
'The sun'—you see his scribble—'does not move'.
Strange how that fantasy of thought recurs
In Plutarch's pages, these, and Kopernik's!
This note? 'Tears come from the heart, and not the brain.'
There, tediously he argues light is wavelike . . .
And here the child in Leonardo draws
Silk canopies that open, float and fall,

With men beneath them. These flat, turning screws
Hold hovering in the air uncouth machines:
This, from the hand that painted the 'Last Supper'!
You saw it in Milan? What drama there
In those tense, pointing groups! Only a Sophocles,
A dramatist (I say) could judge that picture.
How patient in the margin smiles this angel!
Notes on birds—there is nothing here to keep us;
And men equipped with wings—
'This seems my destiny, that all my life
I talk of wings.' Wings! And a dozen drawings,
All without beauty. Then, 'The Po will lay
Land down in the Adriatic, as its silt
Formed Lombardy.'
Guns, multi-barrelled—armoured vehicles crawling—
But submarine warfare he 'will not divulge'—
Men are too evil!
So, craft by craft, notes, drawings, diagrams
Disclose the squandered years. 'Trifles,' we call them;
Yet here and there, among these random notes,
We glimpse his style . . . for instance, 'Knowledge is
The natural desire of virtuous men'—
But not of women, no?
'Ere anything is loved, first you must know it,
And even as your knowledge deepens, love
Strengthens.' Here: 'Nothing perfect is achieved
Without great suffering' — ah, those words appeal to you?
I have another volume, full of wit
As these of drawings—your pardon, while I fetch it."

The door closes, and he is gone. How coltish,
Set by these drawings, seem those lines I wrote,
Embroidered with the shapes of burning Troy,
Long since for my Lucretia; lip and eye
Ensconced far less variety of passion
Than this head, that, and all these kneeling figures;
This girl too, leaning on the wind; and here
A felon who had reached the scaffold-foot,
Lighting, or rather stumbling from his horse;
Young, full-cheeked warriors blustering on their way
To Anghiari—theirs, no grey approach
To the white silence; and this boy, whose mouth
Laughs at another's raillery, but his eye
Puckers with pride discomfited: how often

My lips knew such a smile, until that day
When, as I smiled to mask a hurt, I found
The smile true, my heart careless as my face.
What wealth here, gathered from unnumbered walks,
From mornings when he watched, in square or village,
Men laughing, talking, falling to quick blows
One with another, and set them in his book—
Work endless as my own, since like the housewife's
The poet's task is never done: chance thoughts
Insisting on attention at all hours;
The mind's confectory of scene and speech
And dishes spiced for taste with voguish quirks—
Done in my kitchen, in that orchard-plot
Under the Stratford windows. Easier there
Than where the stage brawls or the tavern hums:
Yet what, without those, of my art? What means
Better than they, to sinew the loose will
Until performance marches with desire?
So fantasy must drink a brief delight,
Curtailed by action; and imagination
Feed grossly on the broad leas of the world:
No silk-worm wit, spinning a fragile thread
Off none but mulberry leaves. Fretted and galled,
Hour after hour; yet even in that vexation
More to be learnt than lost; and how complain
Of chafing, when the combed and mincing spaniel
Sulks, but the beggar's, flea-diverted, runs
The livelier mongrel for his bouts of scratching?
Or blame the theatre, to the craft of verse
An hourly enemy, a lifelong friend?
    For me, one craft or art; but what of his
Whose hand scribbled this page, where flowers, hair, arms,
Jostle basilicas and bronze designs?
And now this note—what is it?—"Make a glass,
To see the moon enlarged"; then, "Earth's a star
Like all the rest"; and here he disallows
Their agelong jurisdiction over men . . .
Tiered crags, slow-crumbling: strange, beside the oxlip,
Violet and rose of my capricious love,
That scope of his, which in a landscape saw
The antique force and rhythm of the world;
Beneath the modern turf, the twisted rocks,
Shaped when, unseen, Time like a child at play
Toyed idly, building and unbuilding hills, too young

For hearts and kingdoms: Leonardo's world
Sketched with this subtly smiling woman—peaks,
Blue, bald and sharp, above primordial meres
Where the tailed reptile lurched whose ribs he found
Vaulting with more than stone the cave's damp roof.
Yet eager enough my love was, where the current
Curved and re-curved below the bridge, or brooks
O'er-greened themselves with soft grass lazily trailing,
Till April's breath made all the stream seem flowers;
And harsh the disillusion of the boy,
A breathless truant, clambering through the dingle
Where once the rose-hips laced the burnished blackthorn,
Scarlet amid the purple: there to find
The wild rose-sapling choked and dead, and taste
Time's ancient bitterness. Awhile, religion—
Too early met, too soon embraced, that conflict
Mustering to war with sin those ripening powers
Whose business was to feel, remark, conjoin:
Brief, yet what else had fathered such unlove
For twilight borderlands of light and dark
Where good walks masked, and evil takes her name?
Then older scrambling: sun-burned idleness,
And fancies born of moonbeams, on that night
Alone in Arden, shimmer and rustle and flicker
All night beneath the oaks, until I marked
A violet's blue, and knew the dawn had come;
Dawn-wanderings with the forester, with eyes
That could not take their fill of flowers, nor ears
Of song, nor hands of dew, hands with warm palms
Insatiable for dew and leaves. What touches
Beguiled young fingers: hide, or hare's wet flix,
With the chase ended; down of dove and cygnet;
Furred moss: all those, until I learnt with Anne
How flesh was made for flesh; how her unrest
Equalled my own; and how, beyond believing,
Tumult so great could issue in such peace.
And so began the novel, sensuous months—
Outside, the seasons; and for me at home
The brighter April of her nakedness;
Journeys unguessed, more poignant to the sense
Than wild thyme odours in a windless dell;
And what were the flowered hills, to hands that scaled
The new peak of her smooth-ascended breast?
Strange evening, when I spoke for her the lines

Which first lent majesty to English verse—
"Thence come we to the horror and the hell,
The wide waste places, and the hugy plain"—
And so from rhyme to rhyme, till at the end
The music had no meaning but her body,
And yet the echoing of the harmony
Remained beyond our severance. Wild but harmless,
Our love together: unlike that later woman,
Those sallow cheeks, black mournful eyes, and body
Coarse with a gipsy's lust; adroit to rouse
And fan lust's thick and secret earnestness;
Lust that like Time degrades each thing he touches,
Each innocent thought and purpose of the mind
Besmirched by that invasion, like a slug
Trailing his soilure through the dew-hung blades.
My viler Lesbia: mine, and his, and all men's:
Until that worse discovery of Columbus,
The second and the deadlier, poxed her blood.
Love poisoned, loitering lust, and the long pity
That watched her degradation: what remained,
What that I missed, which should have served for cleansing?
That ulcer I forbore to suck, but left
To film and suppurate beneath the skin—
Did I not know the remedy? Not enough,
Those sonnet rhymes, to heal and exorcise—
"Who taught thee how to make me love thee more,
The more I hear and see just cause of hate?"
But from that sigh, that first perplexity,
Had I but snatched hints of that pair who found
In kiss and clip the nobleness of life,
Yet learning hour by hour, as we two learnt,
Learning how time endures, eternity passes—
Was there in that no remedy I missed?
None, to have made that serpent of old Nile
Beguile him to the very heart of loss,
Yet the world's snare be scaped that trapped us once?
And in her dying, lust be seen transformed
From the hot hands and whisper in the dark
To wonder and to majesty? Would not this, accomplished,
Have out-soothed opium, purged and expiated
More than the hermit's fifteen thousand nights
Within the secretest cave? And for the rest,
My puzzled jealousy, and slow-paced heart
Which ever found more evil than it guessed—

95

Was there no tale at hand wherein to give
All my mistrust of her, so deeply founded,
Proved and re-proved so often, to another
Whose need was only to believe, and love?
Othello—and, distastefuller, his traitor.
      Such were the tasks I shrank from: and what more?
      This man, with fingers subtle as his brain,
Easy for him to suit every notion
Its proper science and particular art:
Apt and prepared to cipher out the bonds,
Infrangible and airy, of the spheres,
Or, seeing a gesture, paint it: but for me,
With my one craft of verse, of stage and verse,
What way but the one to body forth a world,
What but the stage, with all my seen, heard, known,
All blent in turbulent images of life—
Most richly, through the tragic actor's lips?
      The way, then, of the poets. Yet to re-live
The very waste and refuse of our days;
New-act his falsity, let the tongue curl
Around the ruins of her name, revive
Her perjury in another; to renew
This memory or that, guilt done or suffered—
Creep into minds of those who fall asleep
In the contriving of new villainy
And wake to do it; and the rottenness
Which maggot-like works in currupting brains—
For the play's sake to lodge it in our own,
Bid breed and ramble and proliferate
The hate that struck us and the greed that stripped,
External once, now inward; till all good things
Drown in their contraries, and simpering matrons,
The silvered pate and green virginity
Convert to general filth: what's this to any poet
But grief superfluously renewed, a torment
Fit for the damned?—that "suffering" of da Vinci!
—Far easier to abstain!
      And yet those envious wills, plumed up to evil—
Regans, Iagos, Edmunds—would they not
Muster against them countervailing virtues?

Wolves of the state, whose discipline was riot—
Untuners of all harmony—to meet them
Was there at hand no else—unpublished valour,
No strength of loyal hearts pregnant to pity?
With all else beaten, no peasant to stand up
And with a rough hand guide the blades of justice?
Beside self-ruining evil, how fail to set
The unruinable good: Iago undone at last
By the simple goodness of a wanton woman;
Lear, when his pomp had taken physic, finding
Grained friendship, varnished by no flattery?
And with the tempest blown out in the mind,
Trailing its rainbow, was there then no place
For some contingent and precarious peace,
Some glimpse of vice that kneeled to be forgiven,
And in the scope and range of character
Some sweet contagion from the best to worst?

     Character; what beyond it? What of the powers
Unknown, that use us as we use our hands;
Or—if no powers — the casual tragedy
Which makes us guess them? Fortune that benets
What nature failed to infect? And for religion—
But what of his, the author of these drawings?
No heretic?—yet these sharply-twisting curves,
That rage of water, sketched a hundred times,
Towns gulfed in deluges, and huge crags lurching—
What purpose, but to show the whole of nature
Aswirl with random ruin and uncontrollable?
Then the tired sadness of this smile, where shadow
Half hides the cross, and even the saint's hand makes
A gesture into darkness.—Where's He then,
The footstep on the hills, Whom to be near
Was to be near the fire; Whose way of thought
Forged His bright speech to figure, tale, and scene,
Yet for no stage? As in da Vinci's art,
So with those tragedies: there was no call
To bate my doubts: better to have them spoken,
Put questions to the questionable universe;
Ask why earth's teeming and envenomed womb
Breeds the hard hearts that bruise us; why men fall,
Undone by goodness; search what cause in nature
Makes all oblique, nought level in our lives;
Nor shun that misery, when like a play

Botched out by others, with the author dead,
The soiled world hints of some remote creator,
All good, who died with half his work to do.
    What toil, pain, in the writing! But afterwards
Would not the mind discard the uttered horror,
Achieving with freed thoughts its own purgation?
What ailed me, failing to expel the taint
And whiff of those recurrent images
When the ulcerous and distempered flesh of man
Stinks with similitudes of hearts and nations,
Invisibly corrupted? Nauseous foods,
Stale, furred, and greased, re-gorged as soon as eaten—
To end their likeness to long-mumbled love,
Faith offered and profaned, were there not lips
Ready to speak my cleansing? And the animals
Ravening in my head—wolf, bear, and tiger,
Starved, lecherous, faithless—images of man
Preying for ever on himself—dispark them
From my fenced brain, give them a theatre
To struggle and growl their worst in, on Lear's lips,
Iago's, or Macbeth's? The world's roundness
Stamped flat for sin; or, gaping wide in war,
Soldered with shapeless bodies of the slain—
What thoughts to keep, which others should have uttered!
Othello, Antony, Macbeth, and Lear—
There, beyond Hamlet and the woes of Troy,
There should have been my task; worst suffering too; but there
The stern fulfilment of those torturing years;
And after, with the double anguish past,
Who knows what silence and tranquillity?
    So, there was my failure; yet, had I succeeded,
Who would not say,"Of course"? Yes. I can hear them—
"Why, to be sure: tragedies come to Will
As naturally as leaves do to the tree."
And I, would I have thought
Upon the how and why of my success?
Seen, as I now see, where I turned aside
From Marlowe's path: Marlowe, with love of grandeur
For grandeur's sake, not stumbling through a mist
Of fear and pity and love? Would I have traced
My work emerging from the slow conceit,
From overlaboured rhymes of hunt and rape,
Filing of sonnets, to quick verse, and thoughts

That do not come by thinking, spoken freely
In passion or in laughter on the stage?
Changes unthought-on, since in one who works
Sure of his final goal, his art withers—
Uncertain of its end, goes on for ever:
The better, as he learns to subjugate
That instinct toward perfection, which—obeyed—
Redeems the small work but restricts the great:
Bold to accept the faults that grow in scale
As the work grows, passing the meagre bounds
Where the cool craftsman still can reconcile,
Each with each, gloss and mortised into one,
All of his aims and ends: reckless, as Virgil
Superb in a single speech proved Dido right,
Gods and Aeneas wrong—had he himself,
Bound on his epic quest, enraged some girl who loved him;
Then shame, and memories of a Roman room,
Wrote his best speech, subverting all his plan?
And the girl lives, nameless and yet for ever.
        But no Aeneid's mine; and hopeless now
To seize again those scenes which hummed about me
In Stratford, once, and London; now my invention
Heeds them no longer, as the nightingale
Trills undisturbed by some familiar ghost.
Too late for verse more ample, and less prose:
Prose that at poignant issues is to verse
Skim milk to cream. Idle my skill in it
By what I've missed at the other; idle too
Those tales, new-fashioned for my latest plays:
Brisk-witted, bodying forth the quick o' the time;
Comedies with that twist of disillusion,
Not done (as it were) in earnest with the world;
Unsure of feeling, though secure of art,
Plays that deploy their scenes and characters
Like practised squadrons, ordered and adept,
Charging as one, at drill or to a skirmish:
How different from some vaster battlefield,
Where the cool strategy that ranged the ranks,
Bade this wing wheel, and that draw back, devised
The whole course of the battle like a map,
Must watch the sharp design fray and dissolve
Into a thousand desperate decisions
Far in the dust and smoke of headlong war—
What matter, if the battle's won? For me,

No battle now, no clangour of the trumpets
Spurring the will and blood: rather the thought
Of some old legend of Prince Lucifer
Lamenting most of all, of heaven's lost joys,
Clear at the daybreak from the battlements
The pealing of the trumpets.
                                    But why think
Now of that other life, that task declined?
Better to recollect that cripple, pausing
To rest his foot this morning in the square,
The old peasant, with his brown Italian skin
Tight on his ribs, filmed eyes, and cheeks so fallen
My pity made me watch, till of a sudden,
Moved by some inward happiness unguessed,
His lips pursed in a whistle. Luckier far,
Why waste more than a shrug on things undone,
Or, as I turn da Vinci's pages, dream
How, had I chosen, I might have left a name
To be named with his. Lucky it is for men,
Though we grow old, and all around us find
Less and still less to move us to delight,
Each of us has himself to laugh at still.—
But now the old man has found his manuscript;
There is his step, his hand upon the door.

Index of Titles and First Lines